Accessible Text File
How to Prepare Government Contract Proposals
US Small Business Administration
Office of Government Contracting and Business Development
February 2014

Slide 1 How to Prepare Government Contract Proposals

US Small Business Administration

Office of Government Contracting and Business Development

February 2014

Narrative

This is about preparing proposals that win federal contracts.

Welcome to SBA's training module, How to Prepare Government Contract Proposals.

Slide 2 Introduction

- Course is comprehensive with multiple sections covering a variety topics that define proposal preparation

- About building an ***amazing story*** that touches all components of a contract proposal – *such that a compelling case is made for a firm – your firm -- to be the best solution*

- Indexed so the user can easily go forward or back to any section at any time

Narrative

The information presented is straight-forward and comprehensive. It includes multiple sections covering a variety of topics that define and explain proposal preparation.

The course is about building an amazing story that touches all components of a contract proposal – such that a compelling case is made for a firm -- your firm -- to be the best solution.

Importantly, the material is also indexed so you can easily go forward or back to any section at any time.

Slide 3 Course Contents

Narrative

Key topics in this training include: instructions on building a foundation; an overview of the types of solicitations and Standard Forms used by the government; a frank discussion about how to write a proposal; costs and pricing guidelines; the benefits of learning from others; a menu of helpful resources; and finally, a push to apply what you have learned.

Slide 4 Learning Objectives

- Understand the types of solicitations and contracts used by the federal government

- Learn how to respond appropriately to government solicitations with proposals that enhance your chances of winning a contract

Narrative

The objectives for this course are simple and two-fold: (1) to help small businesses understand the types of solicitations and contracts used by the federal government and, (2) to learn how to respond appropriately to government solicitations with proposals that win contracts.

Slide 5 Expectations

- Many companies aspire to do contractual work for the federal government, most will not…

- Many reasons – some firms are not qualified, some are not competitive, some will just talk about it, and others just don't understand (or are intimidated by) the proposal process

- Best preparation is learning about and understanding the process, aligning skills with needs and following-through

Narrative

But first, a statement about expectations. Many companies aspire to do contractual work for the federal government. The reality however, is most will not.

There are many reasons for this. Some firms are not qualified, some are not competitive, some will just talk about it, and others, well they just don't understand how to prepare proposals that get attention and win contracts. It is also true that sometimes the government doesn't buy the types of goods and services you sell, or in quantities that make it feasible for you to bid.

Expectations don't always match reality. The best preparation for winning government contracts is understanding the process, aligning skills with needs and following-through. In other words, prepare, align and execute – that will help you beat the odds.

Slide 6 Building the Foundation

Narrative

Part 1. Building the foundation.

Slide 7 Building the Foundation

- Define what you do

- Register in the System for Award Management (SAM), including the Dynamic Small Business Search (DSBS)

- Develop a compelling small business profile and capability statement

- Find contract opportunities

Narrative

The first step in proposal preparation is building a solid foundation.

A foundation that includes defining what you do in government terms, registering in SAM, the government database of potential and existing federal contractors, developing a compelling small business profile and capability statement, including a Dynamic Small Business Search profile and finally, finding contract opportunities that are suitable for you to bid on.

This is all preliminary before preparing a contract proposal for the government….

If you are new to the government contracting space, consider reviewing the 3-part GC 101 training series. This series will provide you with an understanding of contract basics. You really do need to understand the basics, before you can appreciate how to prepare a contract proposal.

Slide 8 Define Your Products and Services

- Government/firms use the North American Industry Classification System (NAICS) to identify products and services

- DOD uses Federal Supply Group and Class (FSG/FSC)

- D-U-N-S numbers are used to identify prospective vendors

- Commercial and Government Entity (CAGE) code used to identify a contractor's facility at a specific location

Narrative

The government is a unique buyer. Federal agencies use the North American Industry Classification System, more commonly referred to as a NAICS code, to identify products and services by industry type. The NAICS code is a six digit number that describes or defines a particular product or service a company supplies. A firm will generally have a primary NAICS code, but can have multiple NAICS codes as well.

You can find and define the NAICS codes for your products and services by using the referenced hyperlink. It is also important to note that you can use your NAICS code or codes to conduct online searches at the websites of numerous federal agencies to learn what they are buying. A NAICS code, or codes, identifies the products and services your company supplies. It does not uniquely identify your business. The Federal government uses D-U-N-S numbers, provided by Dun & Bradstreet, to identify prospective vendors. You can obtain a D-U-N-S number at no cost to you by clicking on the hyperlink.

To participate in contract opportunities within the Department of Defense, a firm will also need to know its Federal Supply Group or Class code. In addition, the Commercial and Government Entity or (CAGE) Code is a five-character ID number used extensively within the federal government. The CAGE code is used to support a variety of mechanized systems throughout the government and provides a standardized method of identifying a given facility at a specific location.

Slide 9 Register in SAM

- The System for Award Management (SAM) is the primary source for agencies to learn about prospective vendors

- Government maintained database

- A firm must register in SAM to participate as a seller in the Federal space

- Small firms should also maintain an updated Dynamic Small Business Search (DSBS) profile as part of SAM

Narrative

The System for Award Management, more commonly known as SAM, is the primary source for agencies to learn about prospective vendors.

SAM is a government-maintained free database of companies wanting to do business with the government. This database is a marketing tool for businesses and a searchable list of prospective vendors for the government.

A firm must register in the SAM system to participate as a seller in the federal space. Further, a firm's profile in SAM must be updated at least once every 12 months – for the profile to stay active. Completing an accurate and appealing small business profile in the government's SAM system is an important, foundational step in marketing goods and services to the federal government. As such, you should learn as much as possible about the SAM system. That includes accessing the SAM site and performing multiple searches, as if you were looking to hire a firm similar to your own business. Review profiles of businesses in similar areas of expertise and use them as guides when developing your own business profile.

Also, treat your SAM and Dynamic Small Business Profile as your business resume. And, as with any resume, it should be regularly reviewed, updated and strengthened. Importantly, spelling and grammar do matter as they reflect your attention to detail and can form a contracting officer's first impression of your firm.

Slide 10 Develop a Compelling Capability Statement

- Prepare a comprehensive *Capability Statement* outlining management, technical and business strengths – can help in developing a "line card " or brochure

- Statement should include:

    - Specific capabilities and skills

    - Past performance history, with specific projects and value of contracts

    - Awards and commendations

    - Resumes of key management

- Seek feedback and refine accordingly

- Will serve as an important foundational element in the preparation of proposals that respond to government solicitations

Narrative

A business should prepare and maintain a comprehensive-yet concise-capability statement that clearly outlines its management, technical and business strengths. This too is important!

Such a statement should include specific capabilities and skills, past performance history, awards and commendations, and resumes of key management personnel. A contracting officer's time is limited and valuable. A simple one page capability statement is more likely to be viewed, while a 5-10 page document may be tossed on a pile. There's time later on for a more detailed description of your firm's capabilities. Initially, you just want to pique their interest in you. In addition, you can use a well developed capability statement to create a "line card" or brochure that you can use for marketing.

As with your SAM profile, you should seek regular feedback on your capability statement and refine and update it accordingly. Your capability statement will likely serve as a foundational element in preparing proposals in response to government solicitations.

Slide 11 Seek Contract Opportunities

- Find prime contract opportunities

- Find Subcontract opportunities

- Market directly to agencies

- Subscribe to bid-matching services

- Use procurement vehicles

Narrative

A key part of building a solid foundation is seeking contract opportunities that make sense or that justify spending the time and resources to prepare contract proposals. This is an important aspect of proposal preparation. A business can waste a lot of time and money responding to solicitations that do not make sense.

Slide 12 Find Contract Opportunities

- Federal government lists contract opportunities online at www.fbo.gov

- Learn more about FBO: User Guides, Training Videos & FAQs

Narrative

Knowing how to find contract opportunities is critical. A key resource is the government's website, Federal Business Opportunities.

To outreach contract opportunities to the public, the federal government operates a robust, online service called Federal Business Opportunities, but more commonly known as FBO or FedBizOpps. This single entry, government-wide website profiles available business opportunities and is one of the most powerful tools available to help a firm become successful in government contracting. The online tool identifies contract opportunities over $25,000.00.

Firms can also view past awarded contracts in the FBO – which may help you with preparing future proposals or bids. This is important.

Slide 13 Find Subcontract Opportunities

- Subcontracting can be profitable

- Performing as a subcontractor can prepare you to be a prime contractor in the future

- SBA maintains a database of subcontracting opportunities. This searchable database is called SUB-Net

- SBA also profiles on its website the Subcontracting Opportunities Directory by state

Narrative

An alternative to seeking prime contracts is to explore subcontracting opportunities.

Subcontracting with a prime contractor can be a profitable experience as well as a growth opportunity for a business. To help small businesses find opportunities, SBA maintains, SUB-Net, a searchable database of available subcontract opportunities. The SBA also displays on its website the Subcontracting Opportunities Directory by state.

At your convenience, return to this slide and use the links to explore subcontracting opportunities.

Slide 14 Use Procurement Vehicles

- Consolidated purchasing vehicles

- Multiple Award Schedules
- Learn about GSA Schedules
- Learn about GWACS
- Some agencies offer agency-wide contract vehicles
- Some Multiple Award Schedules maybe reserved specifically for small firms

Narrative

The Federal government tries to benefit from economies of scale and make it easier for vendors to sell to the government by establishing Multiple Award Schedules.

These schedules are often referred to as procurement vehicles. Two examples of this type of contracting include General Services Administration (GSA) Schedules and Government Wide Acquisition Contracts or (GWACs). Under the GSA Schedule, GSA negotiates prices and terms with prospective vendors and enters into an agreement with those vendors. Under the agreement, participating government agencies can purchase products and services from a schedule of prospective vendors, according to prices and terms already agreed to by the vendors. It is also important to note that some agencies offer agency-wide contract vehicles.

Procurement vehicles can be valuable tools for small businesses to gain access to contract opportunities. Importantly, some multiple award schedules are exclusively set-aside for small firms.

Slide 15 Subscribe to Bid-Matching Services

- Some companies subscribe to bid-matching services

- Provide contract leads that match a client's qualifications

- Procurement Technical Assistance Centers (PTACs) offer free bid-matching services -- find your local PTAC

Narrative

Some companies subscribe to bid-matching services. Such services provide leads on prospective contract opportunities that match a business's qualifications. These services can do much of the work associated with finding contract opportunities, but the business still has to prepare the bid or proposal and win the contract.

It is also important to note that the FBO has a service which can alert you to bid opportunities. PTACs also offer free bid matching services. PTACs, funded by the Department of Defense, can be excellent overall procurement resource.

Slide 16 Types of Solicitations

Narrative

Part 2. Types of solicitations.

Slide 17 Types of Solicitations

- Government contracting is big business

- Bid package is usually a set of documents to which a bidder would develop a responsive proposal

- Solicitations used by the government typically come in three formats

    - Request for Quote (RFQ)

    - Request for Proposal (RFP)

    - Invitation for Bid (IFB)

    - Sources Sought (RFI)

Narrative

Government contracting is big business with thousands of contracts -- in hundreds of billions of dollars -- being executed by the federal government each year.

The bid packages used by the government usually contain a set of documents to which a bidder develops a responsive proposal. Such solicitations typically come in four primary formats or types: Request for Quote (RFQ); Request for Proposal (RFP); Invitation for Bid (IFB); and, Source Sought – Request for Information (RFI). Each of these solicitation types, as well as some of the key forms required by the government are discussed in the following slides.

Slide 18 Solicitation Numbers

- Solicitation numbers are important to understand…….

- **SBA123-14-R-0000**

Narrative

To better understand the types of solicitations, let's first look at the government's numbering system.

Each solicitation issued by the government is assigned a number. The number tells much about the solicitation. The first six digits identify the buying facility. The second two digits indicate the fiscal year the contract was issued in. The alpha character defines the type of solicitation – which is both revealing and important. The R character – shown here -- indicates a request for proposal. The last four digits represent the contract identifier or order number.

The alpha code is further explained in the next slide.

Slide 19 About the Alpha Character

- R   Request for Proposal

- B/I   Sealed bid (IFB)

- J   Reserved

- T   RFQ under $25k

- Q   RFQ under $150k

Narrative

The alpha character or code used in the numbering system is important to understand. Different letters mean different things.

For instance, R is for request for proposal, B is for sealed bid (sometimes the letter I is used), J is reserved, T is for a request for quote under $25K, and Q is for a request for quote under $150k.

Slide 20 Request for Quotation RFQ

- RFQ is informational -- used by the government to obtain information and quotations

- Estimated value of the government's need is expected to be under $150,000 and simplified acquisition procedures will apply

- RFQ may also be used in circumstances where simplified acquisition procedures are not used

- Bid package typically includes Standard Form 18 (SF18)

Narrative

A Request for Quotation or RFQ is the type of solicitation used by the government to obtain information and quotations, but the responses are not considered offers. This solicitation type is typically used when the estimated value of the government's need is expected to be under $150,000 and simplified acquisition procedures will apply. An RFQ, however may also be used in some circumstances where the estimate value of the government's need exceeds the simplified acquisition threshold.

An RFQ bid package typically includes Standard Form 18.

Slide 21 Request for Proposal RFP

- RFP is will result in a negotiated contract

- Proposals are often discussed and negotiated with government buying units and pricing, technical requirements and deliverables are subject to change

- Bid package typically includes Standard Form 33 (SF33) or Standard Form 1447 (SF1447)

- Electronic procurement systems, such as GSA's *eBuy* – offer a fully electronic RFQ/RFP system

Narrative

Request for Proposals or RFPs are used in negotiated acquisitions to communicate government requirements to prospective contractors and to solicit proposals.

RFPs for competitive acquisitions will, at a minimum, describe: the government's requirements, anticipated terms and conditions that will apply, information required to be in the offeror's proposal, and factors that will be used to evaluate the proposal. An RFP will result in a negotiated contract.

An RFP bid package typically includes Standard Form 33 or Standard Form 1447. It is important to note that some procurement systems, such as GSA's eBuy – offer a fully electronic RFQ/RFP system.

If you are unsure of any provision within an RFP -- ask the contracting officer for an explanation. SBA, PTAC and other qualified counselors can also provide helpful guidance.

Slide 22 Invitation for Bid IFB

- IFB is often referred to as a sealed bid solicitation

- No discussions or negotiations – your "bid package speaks for itself"

- Price is key

- Bid package typically includes Standard Form 33 (SF33) or Standard Form 1447 (SF1447)

Narrative

An Invitation for Bid or IFB is often referred to as a sealed bid solicitation. There are typically no discussions or negotiations with the government buying office and the bid package – when issued -- is considered complete for bidding purposes. Among qualified bidders, price is considered the key consideration by the government in awarding the contract.

Responsiveness to the solicitation's terms and conditions are key to a successful bid. Be sure to complete your bid package in accordance with the instructions. Non-responsive bids will be eliminated from consideration.

An IFB bid package typically includes Standard Form 33 or Standard Form 1447.

Slide 23 Sources Sought RFI

- Sources Sought, sometimes referred to as a Request for Information, is an advance notice to communicate to potential bidder firms the government's interest in specific research and development projects

- Used as a market research by contracting officers

Narrative

Sources Sought, sometimes referred to as a Request for Information, is an advance notice to communicate to potential bidder firms the government's interest in specific research and development projects.

This type of solicitation is used sometimes to determine the potential bidder interest or universe for a specific procurement. It is also used as market research to determine whether or not a small business set-aside is appropriate.

Slide 24 Uniform Contract Format – Part I

- Uniform contract format contains <u>four</u> parts

- Part I

    - Section A – Solicitation/Contract Form (**SF 33, SF26, SF18 or SF1447**)

    - Section B – List of supplies & services to be acquired

    - Section C – Outlines or explains the statement of work

    - Section D – Describes packaging requirements

    - Section E – Specifies inspection and acceptance

    - Section F – Describes delivery and performance

    - Section H – Outlines any special provisions

Narrative

For most RFPs and IFBs, where simplified acquisition procedures are NOT applied, the government requires the use of a uniform contract format. This format is described in the noted FAR references and contains four parts and multiple sections.

Part I contains section A, which includes the use of Standard Form 33, Standard Form 26 or Standard Form 1447. In some circumstances it may also include Standard Form 18 – which is a Request for Quotations. Sections B – H include a list of supplies and services to be acquired, the statement of work, packaging requirements, inspection and acceptance specifics, delivery and performance requirements, and any special provisions.

Some of the provisions may only be incorporated by reference. However, you should go to the FAR to read those provisions to avoid any unpleasant surprises later on. Be sure you understand what you will be expected to do if you receive the contract award.

Slide 25 Uniform Contract Format - Parts II-IV

- Part II

- Section I – Contract clauses

- Part III

    - Section J – List of attachments

- Part IV

    - Section K – Representations, certifications and other statements of offerors

    - Section L – Instructions, conditions and notices to offerors or respondents

    - Section M – Evaluation factors and award

Narrative

Part II, section I, contains the clauses required by law or the FAR that govern the specific contract.

Part III, section J, contains a list of all attachments applicable to the contract. And, Part IV, sections K–M include information about representations and certifications – such as 8(a) certifications – required of offerors, instructions, conditions and notices to offerors, and importantly, section M outlines the evaluation factors that will be used to evaluate the award.

All parts and sections of the solicitation are important. However, Section C in Part I and Section L in Part IV are particularly important and should be cross-referenced when reviewing the solicitation.

It is also important to note ----- contract solicitations for bids estimated to be below the simplified acquisition threshold or $150,000 will use a streamlined contract format and may or may not use some of the parts and sections outlined in the uniform contract format.

Slide 26 Standard Forms

Narrative

Part 3. Standard forms.

Slide 27 A Closer Look at Key Standard Forms

Solicitation and Contract Forms

- **Standard Form 33**, Solicitation, Offer and Award

- **Standard Form 1449**, Solicitation / Contract / Order for Commercial Items*

- **Standard Form 1447**, Solicitation / Contract*

- **Standard Form 18**, Request for Quotation*

- **Standard Form 26**, Award / Contract

12

Narrative

To remove some of the confusion surrounding required forms, let's take a closer look at the specific government Standard Forms and when they are used.

Slide 28 Standard Form 33

- Standard Form 33, Solicitation, Offer and Award is the solicitation/contract form used by the federal government, not only to solicit orders, but also to award a contract

- Bilateral document – bidder signs the document and submits it to the government -- upon acceptance of the bid, the government signs the same document and a binding contract is established

- This form is used for either sealed bids or negotiated contracts valued at $150,000 or more

Narrative

Standard Form 33, Solicitation, Offer and Award is the solicitation/contract form used by the federal government, not only to solicit orders, but also to award a contract.

It is a bilateral document, such that the bidder signs the document and submits it to the government. Then, upon acceptance of the bid, the government signs the same document and a binding contract is established.

This form is used for either sealed bids or negotiated contracts valued at $150,000 or more.

Slide 29 Standard Form 1449

- Except in circumstances where an electronic solicitation is used, Standard Form 1449, Solicitation/Contract/Order for Commercial Items is the form used by the government to buy commercial items that are estimated to have a value under the simplified acquisition threshold

Narrative

Except in circumstances where an electronic solicitation is used, Standard Form 1449, Solicitation/Contract/Order for Commercial Items is the form used by the government to buy commercial items that are estimated to have a value of less than $150,000 and simplified acquisition procedures will be applied.

Slide 30 Standard Form 1447

- Standard Form 1447, Solicitation/Contract is used in connection with negotiated acquisitions when simplified acquisition procedures will apply

- May be used in lieu of Standard Form 26 or Standard Form 33

Narrative

Standard Form 1447, Solicitation/Contract is used in connection with negotiated acquisitions when simplified acquisition procedures will apply. It may also be used in lieu of Standard Form 26 or Standard Form 33.

Slide 31 Standard Form 18

- Standard Form 18, Request for Quotation is the form used by the government to obtain information and quotations, but the responses are not considered offers

- Typically used when simplified acquisition procedures will apply

- May also be used for quotation requests that have an estimated value above $150,000

- Standard Form 26 is sometimes used to award a contract resulting from the use of Standard Form 18

Narrative

Standard Form 18, Request for Quotation is the form used by the government – when quotations are not solicited electronically -- to obtain information and quotations, but the responses are not considered offers. An RFQ package is typically used when the estimated contract value is less than $150,000 and simplified acquisition procedures will be applied. Importantly, an RFQ may also be used for quotation requests that have an estimated value above $150,000.

Standard Form 26 is sometimes used to award a contract resulting from the use of Standard Form 18.

Slide 32 Standard Form 26

- Standard Form 26, Award/Contract is the form used by the federal government to award a contract, usually as a result of a *Request for Quotation*

- Similar to SF 33, although it requires additional certification information

Narrative

Standard Form 26, Award/Contract is the form used by the federal government to award a contract, usually as a result of a *Request for Quotation*

In general, this form is similar to Standard Form 33, although it requires additional certification information.

Slide 33 How to Write the Proposal

Narrative

Part 4. How to write the proposal.

Slide 34 How to (actually) Write the Proposal

- Do your homework --- carefully read and reread the solicitation document to clearly understand what is being asked, including clauses and provisions

- If you are not sure about something --- ask questions

- Respond appropriately

- Align your proposal with the government's needs

- Articulate what makes you the best solution provider

Narrative

Just thinking about responding to a government RFP or solicitation can be stressful. Writing the proposal, well that can make you even more anxious.

It doesn't have to be that way. Preparing a response to a government procurement request or invitation is an important task, not necessarily a daunting one. It should be approached with diligence and professionalism.

Writing a successful proposal is about doing your homework, preparing and responding clearly and appropriately, aligning your proposal with the government's needs and articulating what makes you the best solution provider. These elements are critical to successful proposal writing.

Slide 35 Carefully Review the Solicitation and Rules

- Preparation is key – you must be prepared…

- Carefully review the solicitation, including all applicable schedules, clauses, and attachments

- Review and understand the regulations (**FAR Parts**) governing the specific type of solicitation you plan to respond to

Narrative

Preparation is key…

If you are going to respond to a government RFP or other type of procurement request, you must be prepared, or you will likely just be wasting your time. The reality is, if you do not comply with all requirements in the solicitation, your proposal may be deemed "non-responsive."

Carefully read the solicitation, including all applicable schedules, clauses and attachments. This is important. The solicitation is designed to provide prospective bidders with all of the information needed to write a successful proposal. The agency that prepared the solicitation expects you to read and follow it carefully.

Also, make sure you review and understand the regulations (FAR Parts) governing the specific type of solicitation you plan to respond to. Some of the regulatory references relevant to a solicitation and the proposal process are highlighted in this slide. If possible, assemble a team to review and prepare the proposal.

Keep in mind, these are only some references. Other regulatory or policy guidance may be applicable to the specific procurement you are considering. Talk with a contracting officer, PTAC or other counselor for more assistance. Some PTACs and SBDCs offer training on how to prepare and submit proposals. Consider taking such training.

Slide 36 Prepare and Respond Appropriately

- Responding appropriately follows from reading and understanding the government's request

- Answer all questions, provide all information and follow all schedules in the order, time-frame and structure requested

- Business that does not comply with all requirements, may be determined to be non-responsive

- This is important

Narrative

Responding appropriately to a solicitation follows from reading and understanding the government's request. Solicitations are usually very specific and follow a uniform contract format. It is important that you respond, as you are asked – answering all questions, providing all information and following all schedules in the order, time-frame and structure requested. Eliminate any guesswork by ensuring that each response is appropriately identified so the reviewer can readily recognize the section of the RFP which is being addressed.

If a small business does not comply with all of the requirements in a solicitation, it may be determined to be non-responsive.

This may sound like common sense and it is. But, you would be surprised to learn how many proposals submitted to the government that are received after the due-date and that do not respond to what was asked for, or requested. Responding appropriately is important!

Slide 37 Align Proposal with the Government's Needs

- Good proposal will clearly articulate how the bidder can solve the problem or fill the need outlined by the government

- Understanding the government's request is important -- how your firm can execute or deliver an appropriate solution is critical

- A proposal may look good, but if it is not clearly aligned with fulfilling the government's needs, it will fall behind other more substantive, solution focused proposals

Narrative

A good proposal will clearly articulate how the bidder can solve the problem or fill the need outlined in the government's solicitation. This again, follows from understanding the nature of the procurement request.

Understanding the government's needs is important. Even more important, however is how your firm plans to execute or deliver an appropriate solution. It is, after all about convincing a government review panel that your proposal solves a specific problem or need and is the best fit.

A proposal may look good and read well, but if it is not clearly aligned with fulfilling the government's needs, it will likely fall behind other more substantive, solution focused proposals.

Don't get caught up in telling a great story about your company, focusing too much on "we can do the work." What really matters is substantiating how you can do the specific work that is needed.

Slide 38 Articulate What Makes You the Best Solution

- Key is pulling it all together in a proposal package that clearly describes why your company offers the best solution

- No magic bullet – it comes down to doing a lot of things right

- It's about:

    - Understanding the solicitation and responding appropriately

    - Demonstrating how your firm can best fulfill the government's needs

    - Offering pricing that is fair and competitive

    - Making sure your proposal is well-written and error free

    - Showing evidence of success through past performance

    - Interweaving an amazing story throughout all parts of the proposal that makes a compelling case for your firm as the best solution

Narrative

A typical government solicitation requires the bidder to provide a great deal of information. The key is pulling it all together in a proposal package that clearly describes why your company offers the best solution and is the best fit to perform the work. Think capture management……. There is no magic bullet. It comes down to doing a lot of things right.

It's about: understanding the solicitation and responding appropriately; clearly demonstrating how your firm can best fulfill the government's need; offering pricing that is fair and competitive; making sure your proposal is well-written and error free; showing evidence of success through past performance;

and finally, interweaving an amazing story throughout all parts of the proposal, including the executive summary – that makes a compelling case for your firm as the best solution.

It is also highly recommended that you have reviewers outside of the proposal writers to review the draft and final product.

Slide 39 What to Avoid...

- Failure to fully understand the solicitation and governing regulations

- Incomplete or late submission

- Proposal is not specific and to the point

- High on fluff and weak on substance

- Failure to understand best value considerations

- Unrealistic proposal pricing

- Evaluation components are not sufficiently addressed in the proposal

- Errors in the submission

Narrative

Sometimes learning from the mistakes of others provides the best lessons.

With regards to solid proposal preparation, some key things to avoid include: not fully understanding the solicitation and governing regulations; submitting an incomplete or late submission; not providing specificity or focus; highlighting too much fluff and not enough substance, not understanding best value considerations; unrealistic pricing; failure to address evaluation factors; and errors in the submission.

If you aren't selected for a contract, consider asking for a debriefing to learn where you may have gone wrong and what you can do to improve your future proposals. Done in a professional manner, this can be a way to show contracting staff of your willingness to improve and to be more responsive to the government's needs.

Slide 40 Costs and Pricing

Narrative

Part 5. Costs and pricing.

Slide 41 Introduction to Contract Pricing

- Contract pricing is an important aspect of procurement and an important component in developing a strategy to win federal contracts

- COs are responsible for ensuring that agencies purchase supplies and services from responsible sources at fair and reasonable prices

- Firm is responsible for developing a contract pricing strategy that is reasonable, competitive, but profitable

Narrative

Contract pricing is an important aspect of procurement and a particularly important component in developing a strategy to win federal contracts. There are two sides to this issue.

First, the government's perspective. Federal contracting officers are responsible for ensuring that government agencies purchase supplies and services from responsible sources at fair and reasonable prices. As such and to accomplish this, most contracting officers and agency buyers conduct considerable market research to better understand markets and pricing.

A contractor will likely have a related, but different perspective. A small firm wanting to do business with the government is responsible for developing a contract pricing strategy that is reasonable, competitive, but profitable. The typical contract bidder wants to make as much as possible in profit, but at the same time be competitive and win the bid.

As such, with contracting officers doing considerable market research and a high number of firms competing for federal contracts, pricing is an important variable. A variable that can make or break your success in federal contract markets. A business must be aware of historical and current pricing trends, be thoughtful in its pricing analysis, competitive and able to make a profit --- if it wants to succeed in the federal contract space.

Slide 42 Negotiated Contracts vs. Sealed Bid Contracts

- Two key types of contracts

- Any contract awarded using other than sealed bidding procedures is considered a negotiated contract

- Procedures for contracting by negotiation permit negotiations prior to contract award, but may or may not include negotiated discussions

- Pricing a proposal will likely be influenced by your ability to negotiate or not negotiate

Narrative

As discussed in the earlier section, proposal preparation, there are two fundamental contract categories: negotiated contracts and sealed bid contracts. The distinction between the two is important.

The FAR states that any contract awarded using other than sealed bidding procedures is considered a negotiated contract. Procedures for contracting by sealed bidding require the government to evaluate bids without discussions and award to the responsible bidder whose bid, conforming to the invitation for bids, will be most advantageous to the government considering only price and price related factors. Negotiations are not permitted prior to the contract award.

Procedures for contracting by negotiation permit negotiations prior to contract award. However, a solicitation under procedures for contracting by negotiation may or may not actually include negotiations. For example, the instructions to offerors may include the provision, the "Government intends to evaluate proposals and award without discussions." When that provision is used, actual negotiations are not permitted unless the contracting officer determines in writing that they are necessary.

Also and importantly, a contracting officer may request a "Best and Final Offer," but doesn't have to, so be sure your proposal is responsive, accurate, complete and your pricing is fair and reasonable.

Slide 43 Regulatory Guidance

- **FAR Part 15 – Negotiated Contracts**
    - 15.101 Best value continuum
    - 15.4   Contract pricing
    - 15403   Obtaining cost or pricing data
    - 15.405 Price negotiation
    - 15.407 Special cost or pricing data
- **FAR Part 14 – Sealed Bid Contracts**
    - 14.201-8   Price related factors
    - 14.3   Submission of bids
    - 14.408 Award
    - 14.408-2   Responsible bidder – Reasonableness of price
- **FAR Part 13 – Simplified Acquisition Procedures**

Narrative

How you analyze your costs and price your proposal is primarily up to you, as long as you follow applicable government rules and guidelines.

Federal rules for negotiated and sealed bid contracts and contracts that follow simplified acquisition procedures are outlined in FAR parts, 15, 14 and 13, respectively. Also, highlighted in the slide are FAR subparts that are pricing related.

It is important to note, in addition to FAR guidance, other agency pricing guidelines or policies may also apply for specific contracts.

Slide 44 Pricing Approach

- **Product Pricing** (typical formula)

    - Material Costs + Labor Costs + Overhead Expenses + Profit

- **Service Pricing** (typical formula)

    - Hourly Overhead Expense + Hourly Wage + Profit

Narrative

The pricing approach used by bidders for products and services being procured, besides following specific contract rules, is pretty typical, but unique to the business doing the pricing. That is, individual business costs and other considerations are factored into pricing formulas that are typical or generally used.

For instance, with regards to product pricing, a firm would typically consider and add material costs, plus labor costs, plus estimated overhead expenses, plus a profit margin to arrive at a price it would propose or charge for the product being delivered.

Regarding the pricing of a service, a firm would typically consider and add estimated hourly overhead expenses, plus hourly wages, plus a profit margin to arrive at a price it would propose or charge. This type of pricing will require becoming aware of Department of Labor wage rate agreements.

It is important to point out, that some government solicitations and contracts are very unique regarding costs and pricing and specific cost and pricing requirements may apply. Carefully review all government requirements.

Slide 45 Best Value / Lowest Price Technically Acceptable

- Best value procurement

    - process used to select the most advantageous offer by evaluating and comparing factors in addition to cost or price

    - allows the contracting officer flexibility in selecting the contractor who will give the government the best value for its money

- Lowest price technically acceptable procurement

    - process that is appropriate when best value is expected to result from the selection of a technically acceptable proposal with the lowest evaluated price

Narrative

It is also important to highlight the difference between "best value" procurements and lowest price, technically acceptable procurements.

"Best Value" is a process used to select the most advantageous offer by evaluating and comparing factors in addition to cost or price. It allows the contracting officer flexibility in selection through tradeoffs which the agency makes between the cost and non-cost evaluation factors with the intent of making an award to the contractor -- who will give the government the best value for its money.

Regarding lowest price technically acceptable, this is a procurement process that is appropriate when best value is expected to result from the selection of a technically acceptable proposal with the lowest evaluated price. In other word, the contract award will be made on the basis of the lowest evaluated price of proposals meeting or exceeding the acceptability standards for non-cost factors.

Slide 46 Important Pricing Considerations

- Learn from past contracts -- review pricing history

- Consider all costs -- even special requirements

- Factor best value considerations

- Include bidding costs

- Allow for overhead and profit

Narrative

Contract pricing is a critical component in developing a strategy to win federal contracts. A successful pricing strategy will: learn from past contracts; consider all costs -- even special requirements; factor best value considerations; include bidding costs; and, importantly allow for sufficient overhead expenses and profit.

If a solicitation is using a 'best value' approach, the contracting officer may not make an award to the offeror providing the lowest price, rather an award will be made to that offeror who is providing the government with an approach that best meets the government's needs. While price is always a consideration, in a best value scenario it doesn't have to be the primary consideration.

Slide 47 Relationships and the Wisdom of Others

Narrative

Part 6. Relationships and the wisdom of others.

Slide 48 Network – Learn from the Wisdom of Others

- A firm can waste a lot of time and expend unnecessary resources if it doesn't understand how to play in the federal contracting arena

- Knowledge is everything

- Network and cultivate relationships with people experienced in the contracting space

Narrative

If there is one message that is consistent throughout this presentation, it is knowledge is everything. You don't know what you don't know. A business can waste a lot of time and expend unnecessary resources if it doesn't understand how to play in the federal contracting arena.

Learn from the wisdom of others. Others, who have seasoned knowledge and experience in federal contracting. Network, ask questions and cultivate relationships.

Engage knowledgeable people who can help guide you through the challenging aspects of responding to procurement solicitations and trying to win federal contracts.

Slide 49 Building Relationships is Good Business

- Successful business people generally have a carefully developed and cultivated portfolio of relationships

- Building relationships is good business

    - Network - Learn from the wisdom of others

Narrative

Truly successful business people don't necessarily have a mountain of contacts whose names they barely know and who are listed in some electronic file. Rather, they have a carefully developed and cultivated portfolio of relationships.

Building solid relationships of experienced contracting professionals is good business.

Slide 50 Resources and Assistance

Narrative

Part 7. Resources and assistance.

Slide 51 Resources and Tools

- Federal Acquisition Regulations

    - http://www.acquisition.gov/far or http://farsite.hill.af.mil (searchable)

- Acquisition Central

    - http://www.acquisition.gov/

- FAR Part 19 – Small Business Programs

  - http//www.acquisition.gov/far – includes all parts

- Code of Federal Regulations (13CFR)

  - http://www.gpoaccess.gov/cfr/index.html

- Federal Business Opportunities

  - http://www.fbo.gov

- SBA-Government Contracting

  - http://www.sba.gov/aboutsba/sbaprograms/gc/index.html

Narrative

Numerous resources are available to assist individuals who are interested in learning more about and participating in government contracting.

Slide 52 Resources and Tools

- Learn more about:

  - SAM Registration http://www.sam.gov/

  - SBA Size Standards ttp://www.sba.gov/category/navigation-structure/contracting/contracting-officials/eligibility-size-standards

  - 8(a) Business Development Program http://www.sba.gov/content/8a-business-development-0

  - WOSB Program http://www.sba.gov/content/contracting-opportunities-women-owned-small-businesses

  - HUB Zone Program http://www.sba.gov/content/hubzone-0

- Local (client) resources:

  - SBA district office http://www.sba.gov/localresources/index.html

  - Procurement Technical Assistance Center (PTAC) http://www.aptac-us.org/new/Govt_Contracting/find.php

  - Government Contracting Classroom (free online courses) www.sba.gov/gcclassroom

  - SCORE chapter www.score.org

- Small Business Development Center http://www.asbdc-us.org/

    - SBA/SBDC Program Office http://www.sba.gov/content/small-business-development-centers-sbdcs

- Women's Business Center http://www.awbc.biz/locate.asp

    - SBA/WBC Program http://www.sba.gov/content/women%E2%80%99s-business-centers

Slide 53 Reflections and Application

Narrative

Part 8. Reflection and application.

Slide 54 Application

- Review , compare and update your small business profile

- Find and study sample RFPs, RFQs and other solicitations

- Chart your competitive position and pricing framework

- Identify potential government customers and needs you can fill

- Select a solicitation you are qualified for and prepare a draft proposal

- Seek, listen, reflect and act on experienced guidance

- You will know when you are ready...

Narrative

Ok, so we have covered a lot of ground and much information has been shared. There is however, a big difference between learning something and doing something with which you have learned. So..., consider this concluding message a push to apply what you have learned. Take these constructive actions:

1. Review, compare and update your small business profile in SAM, the DSBS and your qualifications statement. Then discuss and appropriately refine under the guidance of contract professionals.

2. Find and study sample RFPs, RFQs and other solicitations in the FBO. Practice responding to these requests.

3. Chart your competitive position and pricing framework.

4. Identify potential government customers and specific needs you can fill.

25

5. Still in a practice mode, select a government solicitation you feel you are qualified for and carefully review all aspects of the request. Go through all steps in the solicitation process and craft a compelling case as to why your firm offers the best solution. Review and discuss your draft proposal with experienced contracting professionals.

6. Continue to seek, listen, absorb, reflect and act on the guidance from experienced contracting professionals.

7. You will know when you are ready to formally submit your first proposal to the government.

And finally, if you do not win a contract after submitting a proposal, try to learn from the experience. Sometimes debriefings can be an excellent learning tool for developing future proposals.

Slide 55 In Summary...

- Presentation is about improving the odds

- Thank you for taking the time to learn about proposal preparation

- Please contact us with any questions you may have

U.S. Small Business Administration

Office of Government Contracting and Business Development

800 U-ASK SBA

Narrative

In summary, this presentation is about improving the odds. It's about understanding government contract solicitations and responding appropriately. It's about building an amazing story that touches all components of a contract proposal – such that a compelling case is made for a firm -- your firm -- to be the best solution.

Thank you for taking the time to learn about government contracting and proposal preparation. Please contact us with any additional questions you may have. Also, consider viewing other training modules in SBA's online **Government Contracting Classroom**.

Thank you.

GCBD|joconnor|February|2014|

Hyperlinks Contained in the Course

GC Classroom www.sba.gov/gcclassroom

North American Industry Classification System http://www.census.gov/eos/www/naics/

Federal Supply Group and Class http://www.dlis.dla.mil/hcfsch21.asp

SAM www.sam.gov

Federal Business Opportunities www.fbo.gov

SUB-Net http://web.sba.gov/subnet/search/index.cfm

Subcontracting Opportunities Directory http://www.sba.gov/subcontracting-directory

GSA Schedules http://www.gsa.gov/portal/content/197989

GWACS http://www.gsa.gov/portal/content/104874

Local PTAC http://www.dla.mil/SmallBusiness/Pages/ptac.aspx

Standard Forms SF 33, SF 1449, SF 1447, SF 18, SF 26 http://www.gsa.gov/portal/forms/type/SF

GLS Registration https://eweb.sba.gov/gls/dsp_addcustomer.cfm?imappsystypnm=8ASDB

Access the FAR http://acquisition.gov/far/index.html?menu_id=40

Code of Federal Regulation (13CFR)
http://www.gpo.gov/fdsys/browse/collectionCfr.action?collectionCode=CFR

SBA Government Contracting http://www.sba.gov/about-offices-content/1/2986

Procurement Technical Assistance Centers http://www.aptac-us.org/new/Govt_Contracting/find.php

Personal Financial Statement http://www.sba.gov/sites/default/files/tools_sbf_finasst413.pdf

SBA Size Standards http://www.sba.gov/content/am-i-small-business-concern

Women's Business Centers http://www.sba.gov/content/womens-business-centers

SCORE http://www.score.org/chapters-map

WOSB Information www.sba.gov/wosb

Office of Women's Business Ownership http://www.sba.gov/about-offices-content/1/2895

Small Business Development Centers http://www.asbdc-us.org/

SBA District Offices http://www.sba.gov/about-offices-list/2

www.ingramcontent.com/pod-product-compliance
Lightning Source LLC
Chambersburg PA
CBHW080804290526

45790CB00008B/3585